SCHIRMER'S LIBRARY
OF MUSICAL CLASSICS

Vol. 1820

Cello Music by French Composers

From Couperin to Debussy

For Violoncello and Piano

Compiled and Edited by

OTTO DERI

ISBN 978-0-7935-5223-8

G. SCHIRMER, Inc.

DISTRIBUTED BY

HAL•LEONARD®
CORPORATION
7777 W. BLUEMOUND RD. P.O. BOX 13819 MILWAUKEE, WI 53213

CONTENTS

NOTE

The eleven pieces contained in this album encompass 300 years of French music, ranging from the gamba music of the Baroque period to the impressionism of Debussy. While the technical difficulties encountered in these selections seldom go beyond the intermediate level, the interpretation requires versatility on the part of the performer. The seventeenth century compositions should be played with crisp articulation and an incisive rhythm. The romantic pieces (Lalo, Saint-Saëns) require a rich, full tone, whereas the selections by Fauré and Debussy should be treated with subtlety of phrasing and tonal refinement.

O.D.

1. La Bandoline

François Couperin
(1668 - 1733)

2. Two Old French Dances

L'agréable

Marin Marais
(1656 - 1728)

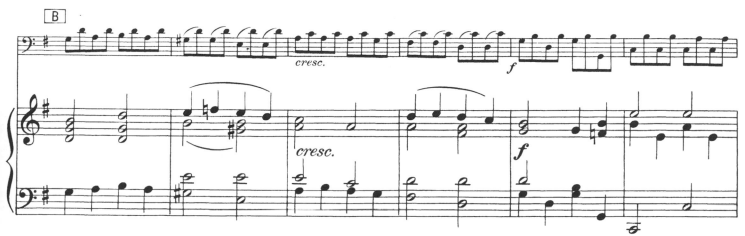

La Provençale

3. La Milanese

Louis de Caix d'Hervelois
(1670 - 1760)

Andantino quasi allegretto

4. Chants Russes

Edouard Lalo, Op. 29
(1823-1892)

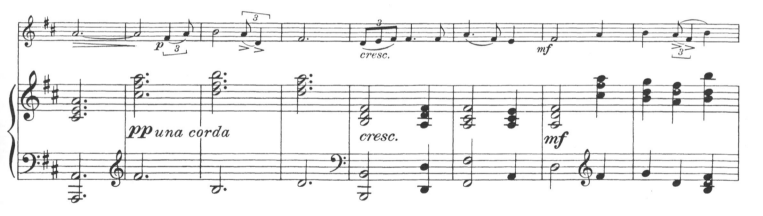

5. Mélodie

Elegy from: The Erynnies

Jules Massenet, Op. 10
(1842 - 1912)

Lento ma non troppo

Tempo I

6. Allegro appassionato

Camille Saint-Saëns, Op. 43
(1835 - 1921)

Allegro appassionato

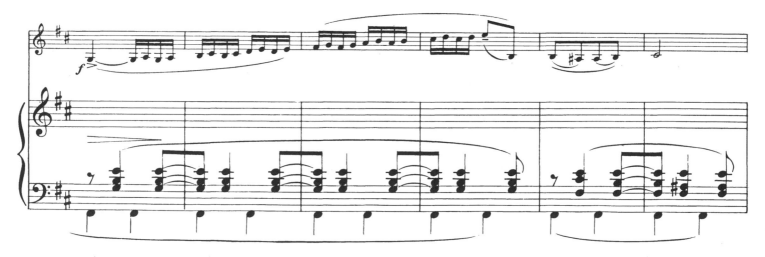

Violoncello

SCHIRMER'S LIBRARY
OF MUSICAL CLASSICS

Vol. 1820

Cello Music by French Composers

From Couperin to Debussy

For Violoncello and Piano

Compiled and Edited by
OTTO DERI

ISBN 978-0-7935-5223-8

G. SCHIRMER, Inc.

DISTRIBUTED BY

HAL•LEONARD®
CORPORATION
7777 W. BLUEMOUND RD. P.O. BOX 13819 MILWAUKEE, WI 53213

1. La Bandoline

Violoncello

François Couperin
(1668-1733)

2. Two Old French Dances

L'agréable

Violoncello

Marin Marais
(1656-1728)

La Provençale

Violoncello

3. La Milanese

Violoncello

Louis de Caix d'Hervelois
(1670-1760)

Andantino quasi allegretto

4. Chants Russes

Violoncello

Edouard Lalo, Op. 29
(1823-1892)

5. Mélodie

Elegy from: The Erynnies

Violoncello

Jules Massenet, Op. 10
(1842-1912)

6. Allegro appassionato

Violoncello

Camille Saint-Saëns, Op. 43
(1835-1921)

Allegro appassionato

Violoncello

11

Violoncello

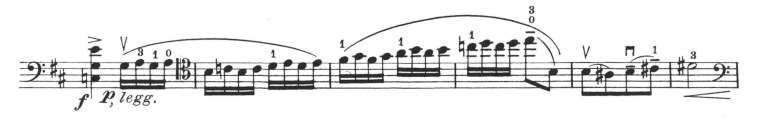

7. Elegy

Violoncello

Gabriel Fauré, Op. 24
(1845-1924)

Molto adagio

Violoncello

8. Papillon
(Butterfly)

Violoncello

Gabriel Fauré, Op. 77

9. Après un Rêve
(After a Dream)

Violoncello

Gabriel Fauré

10. Rêverie

Violoncello

Claude Debussy
(1862-1918)

Poco più animato

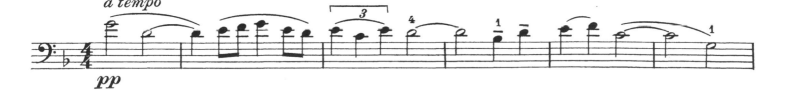

a tempo

11. Menuet

from: Petite Suite

Violoncello

Claude Debussy

7. Elegy

Gabriel Fauré, Op. 24
(1845-1924)

Molto adagio

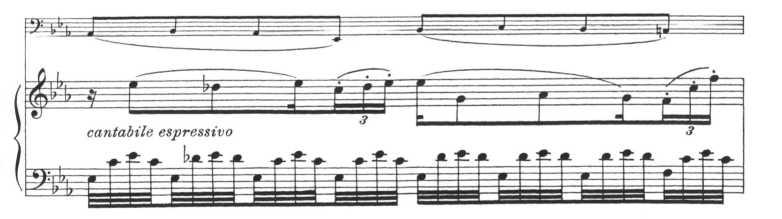

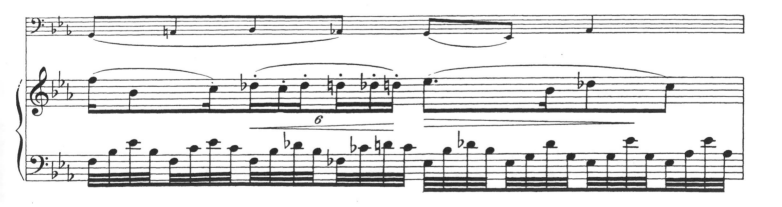

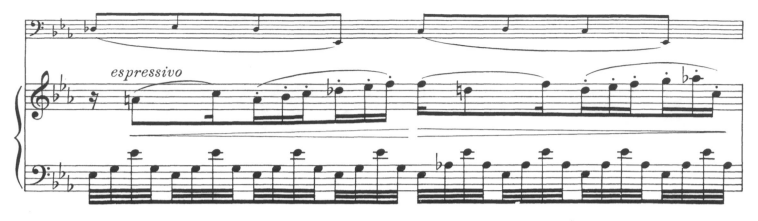

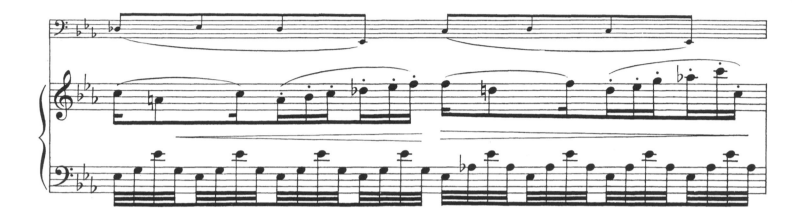

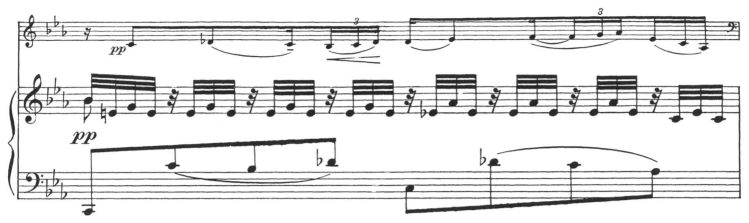

8. Papillon
(Butterfly)

Gabriel Fauré, Op. 77

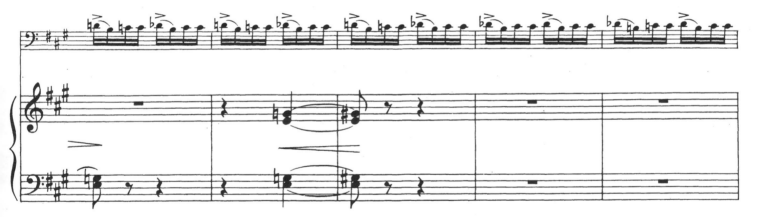

sempre espressivo

9. Après un Rêve
(After a Dream)

Gabriel Fauré

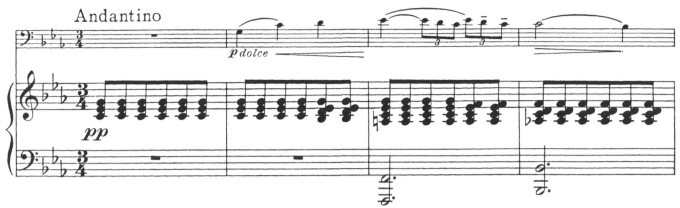

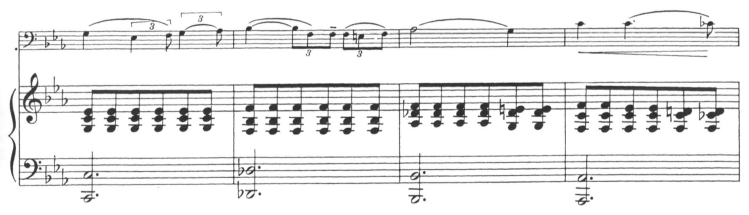

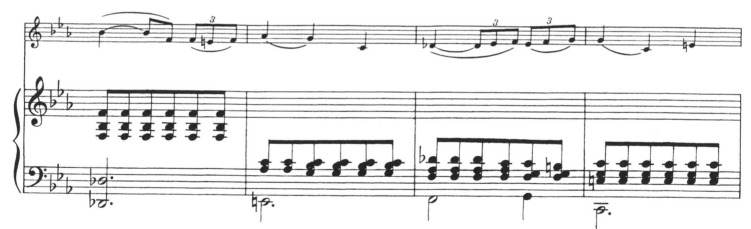

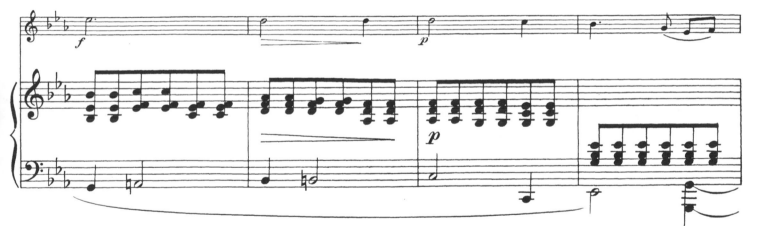

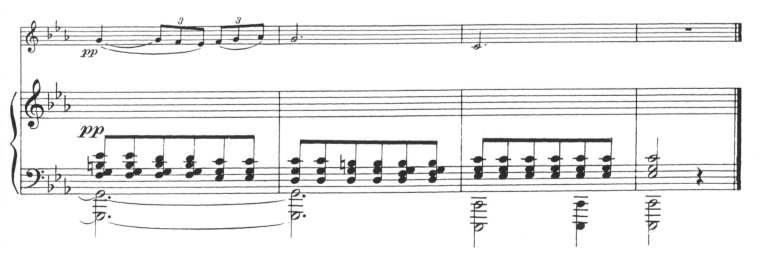

10. Rêverie

Claude Debussy
(1862 - 1918)

Poco più animato

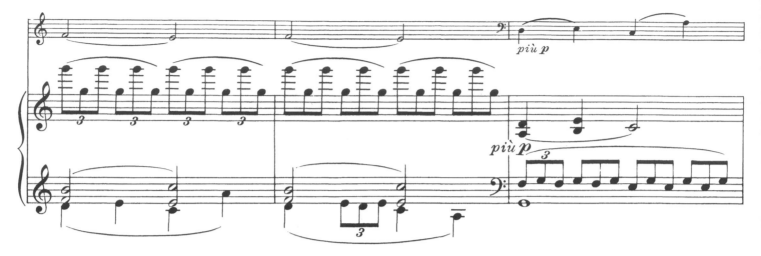

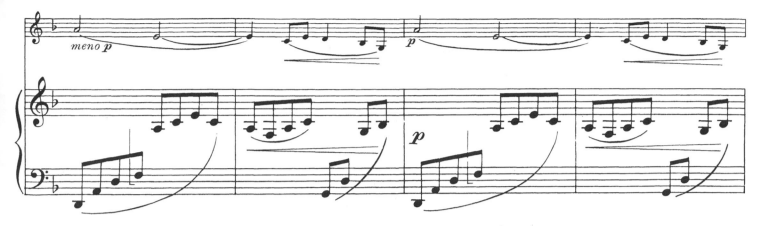

11. Menuet

from: Petite Suite

Claude Debussy

Moderato

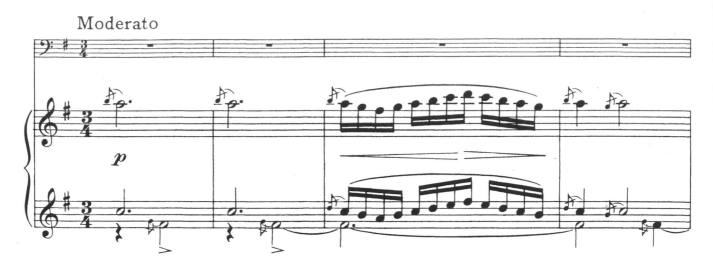

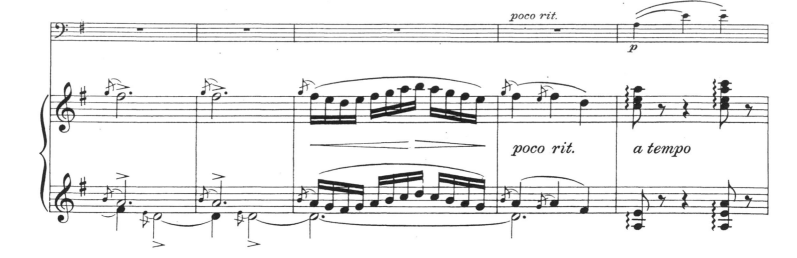

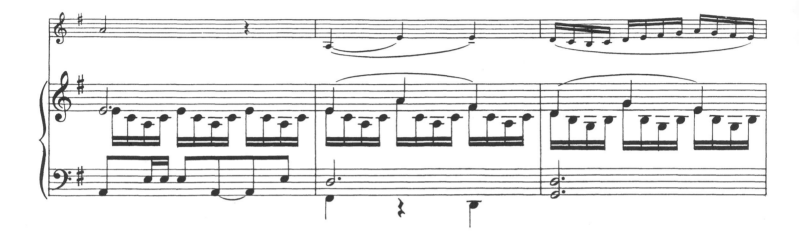

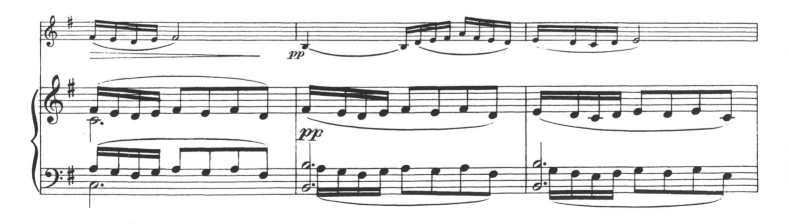